DATE DUE

FEB 2 1 20 2015		
OCT 1 6 2015		
JAN 2 7 2016		
MAN 1 0 2018		

Mechanical Engineering

by Don Herweck

Science Contributor
Sally Ride Science
Science Consultant
Jane Weir, Physicist

McLean County Unit #5
201-EJHS

First hardcover edition published in 2009 by
Compass Point Books
151 Good Counsel Drive
P.O. Box 669
Mankato, MN 56002-0669

Editor: Mari Bolte
Designer: Heidi Thompson
Editorial Contributor: Sue Vander Hook

Art Director: LuAnn Ascheman-Adams
Creative Director: Keith Griffin
Editorial Director: Nick Healy
Managing Editor: Catherine Neitge

 This book was manufactured with paper containing at least 10 percent post-consumer waste.

Library of Congress Cataloging-in-Publication Data
Herweck, Don.
 Mechanical engineering / by Don Herweck.
   p. cm. — (Mission: Science)
Includes index.
ISBN 978-0-7565-3952-8 (library binding)
1. Mechanical engineering—Juvenile literature. I. Title. II. Series.
TJ147.H47 2008
621—dc22   2008007721

Visit Compass Point Books on the Internet at *www.compasspointbooks.com*
or e-mail your request to *custserv@compasspointbooks.com*

Table of Contents

Imagine yourself at an amusement park. You can smell the food and hear the sounds of people talking and laughing. What about the rides? Can you feel the thrill of the roller coaster, the chugging of the train, and the whirling of the spinning cups? Have you ever thought about how those rides are put together and how they work? An amusement park is a mechanical playground, the result of mechanical engineering. It is created by using concrete laws of force and motion.

Mechanics is a field of science that studies motion and what causes it. Engineering combines science and math to design, build, and run structures, machines, and systems. Mechanical engineering is based on the findings of Sir Isaac Newton, an English mathematician and physicist. In 1687, Newton published his findings on gravity and introduced his three laws of motion—Newton's Laws. For centuries, Newton's Laws have been the foundation for mechanics, physics, and many other areas of science.

Amusement parks are designed and built using laws of mechanical engineering.

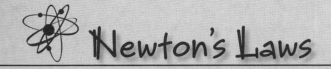

Newton's Laws

Newton's Laws are all about motion and force. The first law, called the Law of Inertia, states that an object at rest will stay at rest if there is no outside force to put it into motion. It also states that a moving object will continue to move in a straight line at the same speed forever, unless a force slows it down. According to this law, you can kick a ball, and it will keep going unless there is something to stop it.

Newton's second law tells us what happens to an object when force does act on it. When a force affects an object in motion, the object either accelerates (speeds up) or decelerates (slows down). For example, when you push someone on a swing, the person and the swing speed up. A force has caused them to accelerate. But if the person on the swing drags his or her feet on the ground, the swing and the person will slow down. A force has caused them to decelerate. Newton's second law is called the Law of Acceleration.

The third law, the Law of Reciprocal Actions, is about actions and reactions. It states that for every action, there is an equal and opposite reaction. Therefore, if force is used, something will happen in response to that force to equal the energy of the force. For instance, if you kick your feet backward while swimming, your body moves forward. You move forward with energy equal to the energy of your kick.

Did You Know?

Isaac Newton's laws of motion made the first flights to the moon possible. His principles helped engineers design modern spacecraft.

Free Fall

When you go to an amusement park, you probably don't think about the physics of force and motion. But you can be assured that the people who built the park thought about these things.

Free-fall rides are a good example. The force of powerful motors raise the vehicle and its riders to the top. The amount of force varies, depending on the size and weight of the riders and cars. Once it is at the top, the real ride begins—a free-fall based on the force of gravity. The riders drop at the same rate of speed and come to a stop in gentle stages at the bottom. If the riders fell to the ground all at once, they would be seriously injured.

Newton's Laws of Motion

First Law
1

Things at rest stay at rest ...

Moving things keep moving ...

unless acted on by an outside force.

Second Law
2

More force means **MORE** acceleration.

More mass means **LESS** acceleration.

Third Law
3

If an object exerts a force on a second object ...

... the second object exerts an equal force on the first.

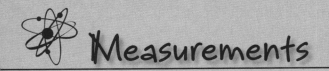

To put Newton's Laws into practice, mechanical engineers must first use exact measurements. Engineers must be good at math in order to design, build, and run things correctly. They need to measure things such as length, time, and temperature.

Each type of measurement is divided into equal parts called units. A unit of length may be a centimeter or an inch, and a unit of time may be a second or a minute. Temperature is measured in degrees of Fahrenheit or Celsius.

Academic Architect

Jennifer Waters is a naval architect and professor at the U.S. Naval Academy. She plans, designs, builds, and runs boats of all kinds. In designing a boat, she must first figure out the exact measurements. She must also figure out how much weight the boat can hold and stay afloat. It is important for her to determine the correct size and place for everything needed to make the boat stay balanced and operate efficiently.

Thousands of businesses and other organizations use mechanical engineers to design buildings, machines, and countless other devices. The U.S. Navy uses mechanical engineers to design boats and ships that will stay afloat and be seaworthy under all kinds of conditions. Their engineers must calculate length, weight, volume, and other measurements to properly build these naval vessels.

In 1987, the Smoot units were repainted on the Harvard Bridge.

The "Smoot Unit"

In 1958, Lamda Chi Alpha fraternity members at Massachusetts Institute of Technology (MIT) received an unusual assignment—measure the length of the nearby Harvard Bridge in "Smoots." One Smoot was the height of their fraternity brother, Oliver Smoot. The bridge measured 364.4 Smoots long.

When the bridge was replaced in 1987, two "Smoot" sections of the sidewalk were donated to the MIT museum. It was also decided that the new concrete sidewalk slabs would be 5 feet, 7 inches long (or one Smoot), rather than the usual 6 feet.

A Real "Ruler"

Some units of measurement date back as far as 6000 B.C. Measurements have often been based on body parts. For instance, England's King Henry I (1068–1135) decreed that a yard was the distance from the tip of his nose to the tip of the thumb on his outstretched arm. The length of his boot was called a foot.

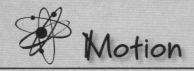

When mechanical engineers design something, they have to calculate motion. This involves figuring out how, where, and why something moves. Engineers have to be concerned about motion because the entire universe is on the move.

Planets in space are always in motion, and Earth moves constantly as it travels around the sun. Everything on Earth is also moving, even the huge mountains that move while Earth turns. From the tiniest atom to planets in space, everything is in motion.

Moving Forward

Motion in a straight line is the simplest form of movement. If nothing gets in the way, there is no stopping, turning, or slowing down an object. It will just go, go, go from here to forever.

Distance, direction, and speed are some things that describe motion in a straight line.

A dolphin moves in three directions. It can travel up and down, left and right, and backward and forward.

Dimensions

Dimensions are different ways things can be measured. Something that is one-dimensional, such as a line, has no width or thickness, only length. Two-dimensional objects, sometimes called 2-D, are flat, like a drawing on a piece of paper. They are measured in length and height. For example, the drawing of a cannonball going through the air is two-dimensional. It moves in a curved line and doesn't move from side to side.

Measuring in three dimensions, or 3-D, uses length, height, and width. Think about a block of wood and how you would measure it. It is three-dimensional because it has length, height, and width.

Using mechanics, a scientist can figure out many things about the line, the cannonball, and the block of wood. Mechanics can calculate their locations, directions, and speeds.

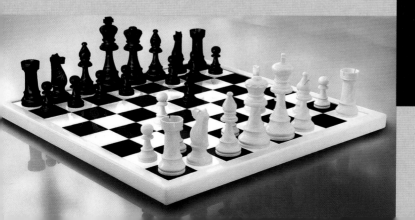

The surface of a chess board has two dimensions, while the chess pieces are three-dimensional.

13

Velocity and Acceleration

Motion involves two important properties: velocity and acceleration.

Velocity includes both speed and direction. It is a change in position over a set amount of time. Velocity is not just how fast something is going; it is also the direction in which it is moving. You have a certain velocity as you drive straight down the road in a car. If you go around a curve, your speed may stay the same, but because your direction has changed, so has your velocity.

Acceleration is a change in an object's velocity—a change in speed or direction. Acceleration is what you feel when a car starts moving from a stoplight. Negative acceleration, or deceleration, is what you feel when a car is slowing down.

Many forces are at work when a cheetah runs and leaps into the air, often to catch its prey. The cheetah's back legs force its weight into the air as velocity pushes it forward. Gravity forces its legs back down. At the exact moment the cheetah peaks in the air, it is balanced between the two forces.

force of leap and velocity

For an object to move, it needs force—a push or a pull. Force can create acceleration, and the amount of acceleration depends on the mass of the object. Mass is how much matter the object is made of.

Objects in motion feel the effects from more than one force at a time. For example, a ball thrown into the air has the force of the arm that threw it. Eventually it is pulled to the ground by the force of gravity. The acceleration, velocity, and direction of the ball change because of the forces at work on it.

Can You Outrun Newton's Law?

Want to run faster? Use Newton's Laws, also called the Laws of Physics. Try bending your arms and legs while running, which takes less force and energy. Now lean forward and let the force of gravity pull you. Remember to lean from your ankles and not your waist. To get the most out of leaning, place your foot down behind your center of gravity. Don't use your leg muscles to press down and back on the ground, because it takes a lot of force to move your weight this way. Use your muscles to pick up your feet, and then let gravity do the work to lower them again.

force of gravity

balanced forces

Rotation

Another kind of motion in mechanics is rotation, which happens when an object spins. A two-dimensional object rotates around a center point. If you spin a sheet of paper on a surface, the paper spins around a center of rotation. A three-dimensional object, however, rotates on an axis. Imagine a spinning basketball, and then picture an imaginary line going through the center of the ball. This axis is the ball's center of rotation.

A Ferris wheel spins on an axis.

The line shows the axis of rotation.

Did You Know?

In 2003, Swiss figure skater Lucinda Ruh set a remarkable record. She completed 115 continuous upright spins on one skate. Her amazing feat involved several aspects of physics, including motion, rotation, and axis.

Basketball Court or Classroom?

A game of basketball uses many laws of physics. The spin a player places on the ball causes a change in velocity, which makes the ball more likely to fall into the net. A basketball player also uses physics to dribble the ball. The hand is the force that slaps the ball to the ground, while the ground reacts to direct it up again. The rubber of the ball and the air inside it help with these actions. Physics even helps a player catch a hard pass, with the player's hands and arms decreasing the force of the ball so it can be caught.

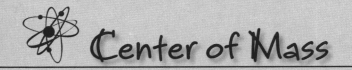

Center of Mass

If you are standing up straight, the spot where you are balanced is probably right behind your belly button. This is called your center of mass. But if you crouch or bend your body, your center of mass changes.

Many things can change a person's center of mass. When a woman is pregnant, her center of mass changes because of the growing baby inside her. She may walk with her body tilted back to compensate for the added weight in front. Her center of mass is now vertically lined up.

If you place a support right under an object's center of mass, the object will stay put, completely balanced. When you sit on a chair, you are balanced on your bottom, your center of mass. It would be very difficult for you to sit on a board placed behind your knees, since your knees are not your center of mass.

Yoga positions require the body to hold its balance at the center of mass.

Snowboarding Physics

To make a perfect turn on a snowboard, you need to remember the laws of physics. To stay up, you keep your body's center of mass over the snowboard. To turn, you lean to the side in a sort of imaginary circle. The amount you lean determines the angle of the snowboard. This angle unbalances the forces and determines the direction of the turn, while the force of gravity continues to pull you down the hill.

Surf's Up!

Have you ever watched a surfer and wondered how he or she stays upright? A good surfer must be an expert in physics, keeping track of the center of mass of the surfboard as well the center of mass for his or her own body. Surfers must also know how the center of mass changes with each movement they make.

Engineers must understand center of mass when building anything. There must be balance; otherwise, the object can never do what it was designed to do. It won't function correctly, and it will probably collapse.

Look at the picture of the juggler on this page. Notice the X on each object being juggled. The X represents the center of mass for each juggling pin. The only way the juggler can toss and catch the pins is to understand the center of mass. If the juggler doesn't understand the center of mass, he will miss the pins, and they will drop to the floor.

The same is true for an engineer. Without understanding the center of mass, an engineer may make incorrect measurements, causing an object to be unbalanced and unstable. The object may collapse when it encounters force.

Center of mass keeps both juggling pins and bridges in the air.

21

Mechanical engineers who design ships, boats, and submarines must understand the basics of physics—measurement, motion, and mass. But they also must understand density and pressure.

Fluids—substances that can flow—add a new set of conditions to mechanics and engineering. In physics, both liquids and gases are considered fluids; they take the shape of the container they are in. Scientists use density and pressure to describe the effects that fluids have on objects such as boats.

Density is a measure of how much stuff is packed into a space. Imagine a box with three pillows in it. The box might be full, but you can probably cram another pillow into a box of the same size. Both boxes are now full, but the box with three pillows has a lower density than the box with four pillows.

Pressure is the force a fluid exerts on an object suspended in the fluid. A boat experiences pressure from water underneath it. A submerged boat or submarine feels pressure from all sides.

Pressure and density also affect one another. A submarine is under a lot of pressure when it submerges, but the pressure increases if it starts moving through very cold water. Cold water is higher in density than warm water, and as water gets colder and colder, its density increases even more. Cold water will push warm water to the surface because warm water is low in density.

In the late 1700s and early 1800s, an engineer named Robert Fulton looked for new and better ways to propel boats through the water. He worked with the properties of fluids to improve water travel. Today mechanical engineers continue this work.

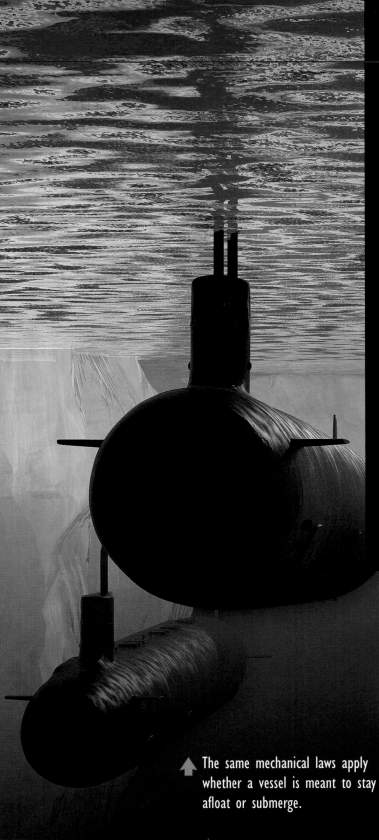

First Vending Machine

The first vending machine was invented around 215 B.C. When a coin was dropped into the slot, its weight pulled a cork out of a spigot. Then the machine dispensed a trickle of water. This machine was built according to the laws of fluid mechanics.

▲ The same mechanical laws apply whether a vessel is meant to stay afloat or submerge.

People have used mechanics and engineering from the earliest times to make life easier. Along the way, some of the world's most important machines and tools were invented.

Long ago, several simple machines were engineered as tools to assist people with common tasks. Many of the machines—including the lever, the inclined plane, the wheel, and the pulley—are still used today.

The first lever was probably just a large stick used to move heavy things such as rocks. Imagine trying to lift a boulder. Impossible. But if you wedge a large stick or board (a lever) underneath it, you can move the boulder by pushing down on the lever. This is much easier than trying to lift the boulder.

Inclined planes also made many tasks easier. An inclined plane works by increasing the distance an object must travel, while sloping the surface to make movement easier. Lifting a heavy box straight up into a

A hammer is a lever when the claw is used to pull out a nail.

inclined plane

moving van can be difficult. But if you slide the box up a ramp (an inclined plane), moving the box requires less force and less effort. Inclined planes have been used for centuries to build roads and structures such as the pyramids in Egypt.

The wheel is another very important invention that allows easy movement of objects. A heavy object can be moved from one place to another by rolling it on something with wheels rather than lifting and carrying it.

pulley →

Another simple machine— the pulley—is just a special type of wheel. A rope fits into a groove along the outer edge of the pulley's wheel. If you had to lift a heavy bucket of rocks, you could tie the bucket to one end of the rope and pull the other end of the rope down on the other side of the pulley. Pulling down is much easier than pulling up, and the bucket of rocks will rise.

Modern Engineering

Through the years, inventions in mechanical engineering became more complex, but they were still based on Newton's Laws.

In 1698, Thomas Savery built the first steam engine to pump water out of coal mines. In 1807, Robert Fulton used an improved version of Savery's design. He designed a steamboat, known as the *North River Steamer of Clermont*, that became a huge commercial and technological success.

The first motorcycle was invented in 1885 when an engineer put a gas engine onto a bicycle frame. That same year, another engineer used an engine to create the first practical automobile.

Human flight was made possible by the engineering of the Wright brothers in 1903. Flight moved into space in this century. The work of many engineers led to modern rocketry for the exploration of space.

1698

1885

1885

early automobile

early motorcycle

first steam engine

Savery's "Miner's Friend"

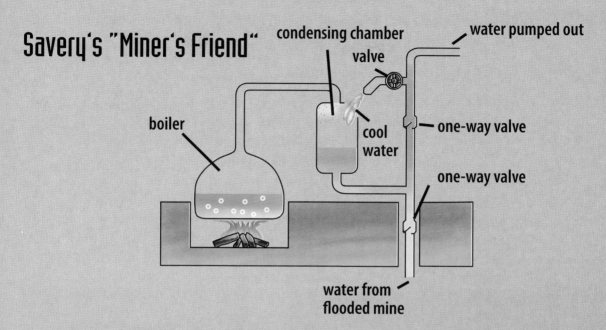

condensing chamber

valve

water pumped out

boiler

cool water

one-way valve

one-way valve

water from flooded mine

Thomas Savery's steam engine pumped water out of flooded mines. When the water boiled, steam moved into a condensing chamber, which forced water up and out of a pipe. Once the condensing chamber was full of steam, cool water was poured on it. The steam inside the chamber condensed into water, taking up less space and pulling water up out of the mine below. Then the process was repeated until the flood waters were pumped out.

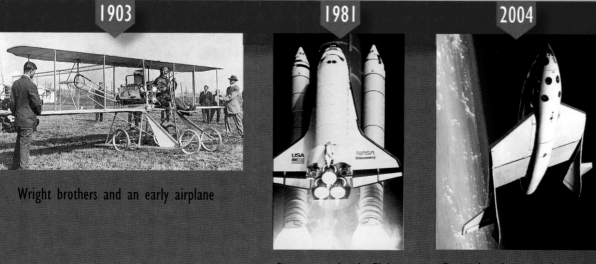

1903

Wright brothers and an early airplane

1981

first space shuttle flight

2004

first privately manned space flight, *SpaceShipOne*

The Future of Mechanical Engineering

In the future, engineers in the field of mechanics will create things we can't even imagine, and many of today's inventions will see great improvements. Scientists also expect breakthroughs in robotics and artificial intelligence, as well as miniaturization, the process of building things smaller and smaller.

The rules of mechanics and engineering—like Newton's Laws—will still provide the basis for these new inventions. Basic laws of motion, force, center of mass, density, and pressure will allow creative engineers to make countless things that will further advance and improve our lives.

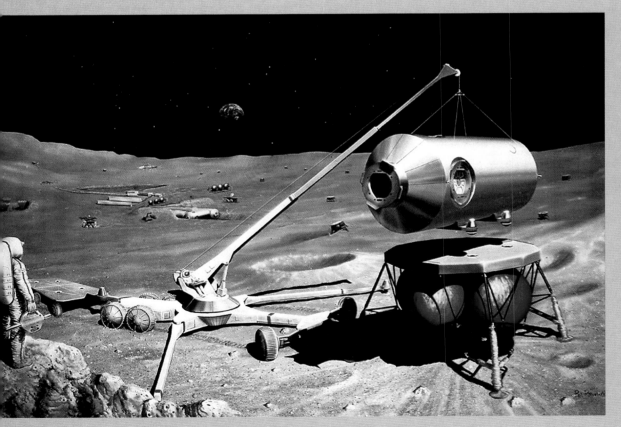

Robotic devices allow us to learn a great deal about space.

Virtual Physics

Video games, as entertaining as they may be, are not purely fantasy. They actually follow the laws of physics. Early versions of video games didn't use physics, but later, virtual reality games used physics software to create an experience as close to real life as possible. Because of the power of newer game consoles and newer computers, games continue to become more and more lifelike.

Game programmers also give "mass" to their objects in the games. In virtual reality, a light object thrown against a heavy one will have less impact than large, heavy objects. This special software makes a crashing vehicle behave more like a real vehicle. Even in the virtual world of gaming, the laws of physics still apply.

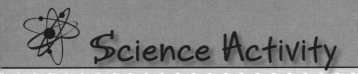

Mechanical engineers must know about the way things work in order to design, build, and run them. For example, a submarine engineer must figure out how to make a boat sink or float. Without this information, the submarine will be useless.

Try this science activity to learn about floating and submerging. You will be on your way to becoming a mechanical engineer!

Materials

- clear plastic bottle with a tight lid, such as a water bottle
- squeeze condiment packet, such as for ketchup
- glass
- water

Procedure

1   Fill a glass with water.

2   Place your unopened condiment pack into the water. The packet should just barely float. If it sinks, try another type of packet.

3 After you have a good packet, fill a clear plastic bottle with water.

4 Put your unopened condiment packet into the bottle.

5 Screw the top on the bottle.

6 The condiment packet is now a "boat." Squeeze the bottle to make your boat submerge, or go downward.

7 To make your boat rise, simply relax your hand.

What Is Happening?

The bottle filled with water has pressure in it. The condiment packet has a small pocket of air in it. When the bottle is squeezed, the air pocket in the condiment packet is made smaller. This is similar to adding water to the ballast tank of a diving boat or submarine. The increased pressure pushes the boat downward. The decrease in pressure brings it back.

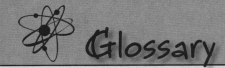

Glossary

acceleration—rate of change of the velocity of a moving object (speeding up)

artificial intelligence—the capability of a machine to imitate intelligent human behavior

axis—straight line around which an object rotates

center of mass—point in an object in which its weight is evenly balanced

deceleration—decrease in velocity (slowing down)

density—relationship of an object's mass to its volume

dimension—measure of spatial extent, especially length, width, and height

engineering—the application of science to practical use

fluid—matter that has the ability to flow and take on the shape of its container

force—factors (like pushing or pulling) that cause something to change its speed and direction

gravity—force of attraction between two objects

inertia—tendency of an object to remain either at rest or in motion unless affected by an outside force

mass—amount of matter a substance contains

matter—particles of which everything in the universe is made

measurement—method of determining dimension, quantity, or capacity

mechanics—branch of physics that deals with motion and the action of force on objects

motion—movement

physicist—scientist who studies physics

physics—science of matter, energy, force, and motion

pressure—amount of force an object exerts per unit of area

properties—quality in a material, such as color, hardness, or shape

robotics—field that deals with the design, construction, and operation of robots

rotation—motion of an object around an internal axis

simple machine—machine without moving parts; designed to overcome resistance at one point by applying force at another point

submerge—suspend an object in water or other fluid

systems—group of objects or units combined to form a whole and to move or work together

three-dimensional (3-D)—having three dimensions: length, width, and depth

two-dimensional (2-D)—having two dimensions: length and width

velocity—speed and direction of a moving object

Cynthia Breazeal (1967–   )
Roboticist who develops socially interactive robots that behave like a friend and rovers designed to explore Mars

Robert Fulton (1765–1815)
American inventor and engineer who made commercial steamboat travel a success; his first steamboat, the *North River Steamboat of Clermont*, made record-setting trips between New York City and Albany, New York

Lillian Gilbreth (1878–1972)
Called the "First Lady of Engineering," Gilbreth experimented with time and motion, and advised several U.S. presidents on how to make work and military defense more efficient; she was the first woman elected to the National Academy of Engineering; her family was the subject of the humorous books *Cheaper by the Dozen* and *Belles on Their Toes*

Naomi Leonard (1963–   )
Marine roboticist who received a "genius grant" of $500,000 to continue her work designing ways to control underwater robot vehicles; her miniature underwater vehicles mimic the behavior of schooling fish

Sir Isaac Newton (1643–1727)
English mathematician and physicist who is called the most influential scientist who ever lived; he described universal gravitation and the three laws of motion that came to be called Newton's Laws; he built the first practical reflecting telescope

Thomas Savery (1650–1715)
English inventor who designed the first steam engine in 1698 and published information about this pumping machine in his book *Miner's Friend*

Jennifer K. Waters (1970–   )
Architect of ocean vessels for the U.S. Navy and professor at the U.S. Naval Academy

385 B.C. The earliest suspension bridges are built in China and Tibet

1620 A.D. Cornelius Jacobszoon Drebbel invents the first submarine, which is propelled by oars

1687 Sir Isaac Newton publishes his work on gravity and the three laws of motion, laying the foundation for classical mechanics

1698 Thomas Savery invents the first steam engine, used to pump water out of mines

1704 Newton suggests a mechanical universe with small solid masses in motion

1769 The first vehicle able to move under its own power is designed and constructed by Nicolas Joseph Cugnot and M. Brezin

1793 Eli Whitney invents the cotton gin

1800 Robert Fulton designs a diving boat (submarine) out of wood and metal, with a hand-cranked propeller that powered the boat under water

1807 Fulton designs a commercial steamboat, the *North River Steamboat of Clermont* to transport passengers between Albany, New York, and New York City

1834	Cyrus McCormick invents the first reaping machine
1860	Frenchman Etienne Lenoir patents the first gas-powered engine
1867	John Robeling begins designing the Brooklyn Bridge, the world's longest suspension bridge at the time; he contracted tetanus after an accident, dying 24 days later; his son, Washington, took over the project; after Washington's death in 1872, Roebling's daughter-in-law, Emily, saw the project out until its end in 1883
1885	German Gottlieb Daimler invents the first gasoline-engine motorcycle, which has an engine attached to a wooden bicycle
1885	Karl Benz, a German mechanical engineer, designs and builds the first automobile powered by an internal-combustion engine
1903	The Wright brothers, Orville and Wilbur, build the first airplane; they fly their airplane on December 17
1914	The Panama Canal opens to ship traffic
1936	Construction on the *Hindenburg*, the world's largest rigid airship, is complete; a year later it burst into flames during a flight, killing 36 passengers and crew members

1951	German engineer Felix Wankel begins development of the rotary engine; the first working model is not complete until 1957
1954	George Devol develops the first robotic "arm" that can be programmed to perform tasks
1957	The Soviet Union launches *Sputnik 1*, the world's first artificial satellite, into space, beginning the Space Age
1981	Space shuttle *Columbia* makes the first shuttle flight that lasts from April 12 to April 14; *Columbia* eventually makes a total of 28 flights before disintegrating in 2003 during re-entry over Texas
1990	The Hubble Space Telescope is launched into space, 44 years after Lyman Spitzer Jr. first proposed the idea
2004	On June 21, *SpaceShipOne* becomes the first privately manned spacecraft to leave Earth's atmosphere
2008	The yet-incomplete Burj Dubai skyscraper in the United Arab Emirates becomes the tallest manmade structure on Earth, reaching the height of 2,076 feet (629 m)

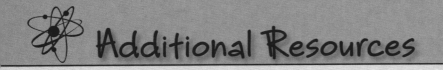

Burnett, Betty. *The Laws of Motion: Understanding Uniform and Accelerated Motion.* New York: Rosen Publishing, 2005.

Nardo, Don. *Kinetic Energy: The Energy of Motion.* Minneapolis: Compass Point Books, 2008.

Rosinsky, Natalie M. *Sir Isaac Newton: Brilliant Mathematician and Scientist.* Minneapolis: Compass Point Books, 2008.

Rebman, Renée C. *Robert Fulton's Steamboat.* Minneapolis: Compass Point Books, 2008.

On the Web

For more information on this topic, use FactHound.

1. Go to *www.facthound.com*

2. Type in this book ID: 0756539528

3. Click on the *Fetch It* button.

FactHound will find the best Web sites for you.

Index

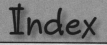

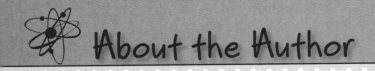

Don Herweck

Don Herweck was born and educated in Southern California and has degrees in math, physics, and physical science. Currently he is an operations manager for a large automotive manufacturer and travels internationally and throughout the United States for his business. He is the father of four children and has recently returned to California after several years living in the South and Midwest.

Image Credits

Sandra Cunningham/Shutterstock, cover (left), 10–11 (back); Shutterstock, cover (right) 14–15 (second, third, & fifth cheetah), 14–15 (back); Getty Images, 2; Danilo ducak/Shutterstock, 3, 23 (back); KB Studio/Shutterstock, 6 (back); Photos.com, 6–7, 7 (right), 10 (right), 17 (back), 19, 20–21 (all); Lisa C. McDonald/Shutterstock, 9 (top); Tim Bradley, 9 (bottom), 11 (bottom), 24–25, 26 (left); Courtesy of Jennifer Waters, 10 (left); Steve Liss/Time Life Pictures/Getty Images, 11 (top); Sergey Popov/Shutterstock, 12; BrunoSINNAH/Shutterstock, 13 (left); Denis Poroy/AP, 13 (right); Corel, 14–15 (first & fourth cheetah); Beth Van Trees/Shutterstock, 16 (left); Dhannte/Shutterstock, 16 (right); Phil Anthony/Shutterstock, 17 (front); Kristian/Shutterstock, 18; Richard Seymour/Shutterstock, 23 (front); Jonathan Cook/iStockphoto, 24 (left); Library of Congress, 25 (top), 26 (middle & right); NASA, 27 (top), 27 (middle), 28; The Granger Collection, New York, 27 (left); Courtesy of Derek Webber, 27 (right); D. Gifford/Photo Researchers, Inc., 29; Nicoll Nager Fuller, 30–31.

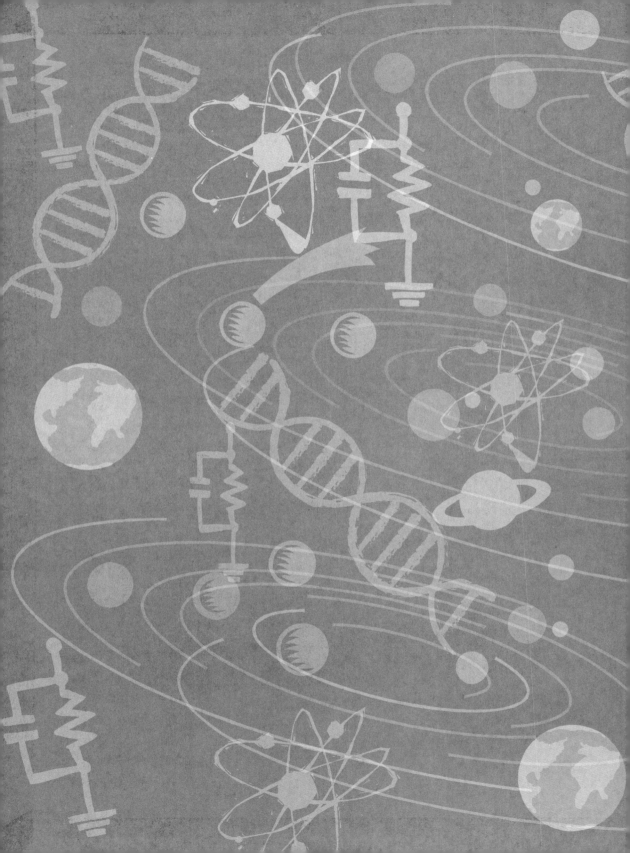